Mistress Carol's

Things you can do with
A Sissy

mistresscarolanne@gmail.com

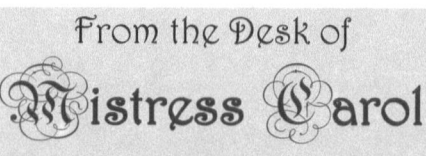

Introduction

To My Dear Mistress, Masters and sissies,

So, you find yourself with your very own sissy to have and to hold. Now what do you do?

In this book you will find information and instruction that will expand your normal hum-drum life with your sissy and transform it into an exuberating day-to-day, fun filled adventure!

Lean to embrace the differences in life and enjoy them. Making a better tomorrow for yourself, through the development and enrichment of your sissy today.

Mistress and Masters will develop a sense of pride in control, a love of challenge and a need to creatively make demands of your sissies that will fulfill many of your deepest secret desires. This is what being a true Mistress or Master requires and can be developed from within you and then proudly displayed to others through the use of your sissy. You should have no fears, no cares, no shame, only the desire to create a true sissy slut that brings pleasure to all whom they may serve.

You are about to experience the life changing words of a Mistress in tune with your sissy, but still, you are the only one that can bring them to the forefront of your consciousness, acting upon them to create reality. You are the embodiment of every sissy's dream, your whims, desires and tasks there's to do at but a command from you.

You have the power to create a heaven on earth within your own personal space; make it so.

Hugs & Kisses,

Mistress Carol

ISBN: 978-1500565732

Printed in the U.S.A.
First Edition

Mistress Carol's
Things to do with a Sissy

Table of Contents

Sissy Basics

So you have yourself a sissy! Your very own personal, living, feeling, caring toy, devoted to you and all things sissy. Well isn't that special, now what do you do?

The first thing you should do is understand some of the basics and identify what type of sissy you have.

Most sissies only have sex with themselves and occasionally with their wives and girlfriends. Most sissies are not very good at sex with females as they masturbate too often, have fantasies that are different from traditional heterosexual relations, often have small penises and have trouble maintaining erections. Various studies have suggested that about 75% of cross dressers are heterosexual; and many gays want nothing to do with sissies. Other studies estimate that of the 75% claiming to be heterosexual, about 50% are probably bi-sexual or wish to be.

Sissies generally fall into two categories. The first and most common sissy has been playing with panties and other lingerie since childhood or early teens. He's really more of a cross dresser than a sissy, since the title sissy implies some degree of service to others, females in particular.

The second type of sissy is introduced to panties, lingerie, and possibly other women's clothing in late teens, 20s or even later in life. The person who introduces him is typically a girlfriend or wife. A few late bloomers discover things on their own, but there are few in this category.

Mostly, a males desire to wear and play with panties and other lingerie is a very private matter that he has not shared with anyone. If he goes off to college or the military, his desires will be suppressed for the time being. Once he is on his own, the desires may blossom or he may just dabble in them, while focusing on dating females. He will likely keep a stash of panties, bras, lingerie, stockings, etc., wear them privately and play with them regardless of his relationships with females. Sooner or later, he becomes involved in a relationship that leads to marriage, living together, or some arrangement that makes storing his stash of lingerie more difficult, but he will manage somehow to hold on to it.

His wife or girlfriend will learn that she is living with a sissy when one of these things may happen: she comes home early and finds him dressed up; she finds him surfing the web and looking at pictures of females with dildos strapped on; she finds evidence of female domination or sissy web material on his computer; she may be looking for something in the attic, basement, or garage and find his stash of lingerie and possibly domination or sissy magazines; disks that contain sissy or female domination images and possibly stories about sissies, etc..

Very few sissies will have the courage to tell you about their desires beforehand. I personally don't know why, because through acceptance you gain control and through control you gain satisfaction. But still, many men fear ridicule and rejection by their wives or girlfriends, not thinking about the day they do find out and what will happen then!

Anyway, if you have caught your sissy all dressed up, keep him that way. If you found his stash, bring it up with him later, in a proper setting. If he is dressed, take him out of the room where you found him and make him stand in front of you while you sit on the couch. Feel free to call him dirty, disgusting, degrading names with plenty of expletives. Ask him directly if he sucks cock or has had anal intercourse with a man. Tell him to pull down his panties so you can see his little tiny worthless cock. Watch his cock's response as you continue to question him about anything that comes to mind. It may become erect or it may be so frightened that it will shrink. Anything is possible.

Make him answer all of your questions. Remember to ask about how often he dresses up and masturbates. Also, how often he shops for lingerie and have him tell you in great detail about everything he owns. If he admits to any male-to-male encounters, ask him how often, does he have a boyfriend or just pick-up guys at various locations. Does he use condoms? Finally, when you are through with your questioning, demand he take you to his stash. You will now take possession of all of his items.

Tell him from now on you will decide when and if he can wear any of it again. That from now on you will decide when and if he may cum again. Lastly, tell him that from now on you will make sure he is properly supervised, so he can't dress or play with himself while you are away.

Store his stuff under lock and key or give it to a trusted friend to store. As you told him, you will decide what he wears and when he may wear it. You will now also decide how, if and when he may cum.

From now on make sure he wears panties all the time. For the most part, they will be full-cut briefs, in pastel colors and get some with flowers and lace too. Go together to a mall or major department store to purchase his panties. He should purchase them, under your supervision, and pay for them on his own. Or, you could take him into the store, openly discuss in the store with the sales staff which ones would be suitable for him and then point to the panties you want him to purchase. He will pick them up and hold them in front of his waist, so that you can approve. Be sure there are other people around to see this. Then take the panties in your hands and stretch it from his navel to the middle of his back. You will hold it there and say loudly enough to be heard, "These panties should fit your properly". After that, let him purchase the panties using his credit card or personal check. Then the clerk can say if she chooses, "Thank you, Mr. ————. I hope you enjoy your purchase." He will respond, "Sissy thanks you for helping him today and he will enjoy wearing his new panties."

From this point forward, he should sleep in a ladies' nightgown that suits you. Pick up two or three when you get his panties using the shame shopping technique.

In addition to wearing panties and nighties, he should use only feminine deodorant, soap, shampoo, powder, lotion, etc. and no aftershave, only a suitable perfume should be used. You should buy this in the same outing as the panties and nighties.

When you get home, have him donate all his male pajamas and underwear, except for one pair, which we will use later. Inform him that from now on he must sit whenever he pees and will always leave the bathroom door open when you are together so that you may verify this fact.

Before you go to bed on this first night of discovery, have him shave off all his body hair. Tell him, from on he will he will keep his body free from all hair and feeling smooth at all times. He will shave or have himself waxed in a salon as needed. Of course, the lady who waxes him will likely learn his secret, especially if you tell her and attend his waxing.

From this point forward, he will address you as Mistress, Mistress ———, Miss, Madam, Madame, or whatever preface you may personally prefer.

I strongly recommend a chastity device for all sissies, as most are compulsive masturbators. Don't be surprised if he masturbates in the office restroom. Until you can lock him up, you may want to have his time away from you supervised as much as possible. To do so, you may enlist help from any female relative living nearby, a trusted friend of neighbor, or whomever you like. They will serve as a "sissy-sitter" when you are not there. If you don't want to tell them why, make up a good story about how he's under a lot of pressure at work, has been depressed lately, or whatever. You just want someone to be around him when you are not there. Let him assume that you told them he was a sissy.

There are many chastity device shops on line that you can order from. An ideal situation would be to have your sissy sit with you while you shop and discuss the various types, advantages, disadvantages, etc. When your order finally arrives, it should be installed as soon as possible. At this point he will be following your instructions to the letter or else you will be telling everyone you know that he is a sissy. Another consequence of wearing a chastity device is that he will always have to sit to pee; you can be assured of it!

Probably, when he starts to get dressed in the morning he will likely complain that he can't wear his panties to work or at the gym. You will tell him that since he wants to play dress up, he will wear panties all the time as women do. It's a good idea to have him wear panty liners or thin pads to catch his sissy drippings. Once he is locked up in a chastity device, pads become even more necessary. Finally, one qualification, if he works in the public safety field and has to change clothes in a locker room, you might consider letting him wear cotton Hanes or Jockey for Her to work. It may make it too difficult if he was found to be wearing really feminine looking panties.

At this point, you now know about your male's desire to be a sissy. You have taken your first steps of control and put him panties and nighties. You have begun his transformation by requiring him to keep his body clean shaven and smooth for you. You have begun to shape your sissy into the model of your perfection.

Over the next day or two just get accustomed to the new changes. Let it all soak in and observe as he keeps up with your new chores created for him. Then add in nail polish. Require you sissy to keep clear polish on his fingernails at all times and work permitting, a colored polish on his toes. This will be the beginning of his total servitude to you and push him into the depths of sissy hood like never before. Now added to his routine, will be keeping his polish up; making sure it is on without chips, changing the color on a frequent basis and touching it up so he always looks his best!

You may wish to have a little ceremony to celebrate that your sissy will be wearing panties from now on. You may wish to invite a close friend or friends to add to his experience. The invitees could include any males, including gay males, who might be sympathetic with your decision.

Sissy will be wearing his last pair of male underwear. Wearing nothing else, he will stand in front of a small table that has two lit candles on it. On the left side of candles will be a pair of scissors, between the candles will be a nice silky pair of pink panties. On your command, he will remove his last pair of male underwear and place them to the right of the candles. He will then put on the pink panties as he states five times,

"I am a sissy and will always wear panties."

When he is through, he will pick up the scissors and the male underwear. He will first cut out the label, which will be saved for lamination and then posted in a place where he will see it daily. He will then cut the underwear into little pieces and deposit the pieces on the table. You will now congratulate him on accepting his sissy status and recognizing the need for him to wear panties. If you have other guests, you may want to serve refreshments while sissy stands in front of the table in his panties and watches. Now is an excellent time to pick his new sissy name. Have your friend participate and make suggestions for your consideration, write them down and maybe vote or draw from a hat.

Another name choosing idea is to have him, as he stands at the table looking at you and your friends, name of some of the girls from high school who really got him excited but would have nothing to do with him. He will mention a few names. Ask him which one he liked best and why. When he has responded and finished his explanation of why, then you can respond with, "fine, your name is now sissy ———." Using the name of the
girl in school he just spoke about.

We all realize that some males want to become sissies. However, your male may not want to become a sissy, but for one reason or another you may decide to make him a sissy anyway! Some of these reasons may include the following:

● If your male thinks it's ok to get into another woman's panties, he certainly needs to be put into his own panties. Locking up his cock becomes a very high priority.

● Being caught with a porno collection that is especially debasing and degrading toward women. This collection may be magazines, on his pc, DVD's, or videos.

● If he has developed a habit of staring too long and repeatedly at other women, or if he has been repeatedly making sexist's comments.

● Any accusation of sexual harassment that appears to have a reasonable amount of credibility.

● Realizing that he has been dressing up in your panties, lingerie and or clothes.

● Not treating you with enough respect or kindness as he should.

● You think there is nothing wrong with having a sissy husband or boyfriend. You prefer it that way!

● You want to have other men and the security of a long term relationship.

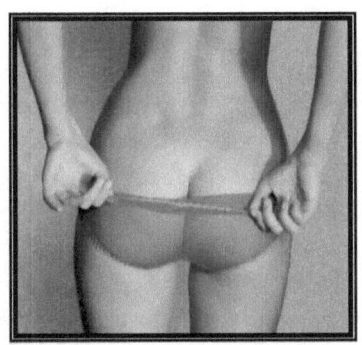

Shopping with Sissy

Now it's time to take sissy, sissy shopping. A good place might be a discount mall that's not too far away. Outlet stores have great prices and they have been known to be sissy friendly which allows him to try on ladies clothes in the store, even bras. Purchasing sissy's wardrobe does not have to strain the family budget. Don't forget about the consignment and second-hand stores. You can find some real treasures there, including great tees and maybe even shorts for sissy. For winter clothes, it is the place to go. Your ultimate goal is to have enough sissy clothes for all seasons so that he will only wear men's clothing to work and when with family. His sissy clothing will occupy the major part of his closet with his male clothes in the back. His dresser will hold sissy clothing only. Even his work socks will be women's trouser socks.

Whenever sissy goes shopping, he will ask for assistance from a sale clerk. He will tell her that the item he is looking for is for him, since he is a sissy. He will thank the sales clerk, "Sissy —— thanks you for helping him today and he will enjoy wearing his new ————." After he had visited the store a few times, the clerks will recognize him and say hello to him using his sissy name.

For bras, it would be nice for your sissy to have a professional fitting. If you make inquiries, you will probably find some lingerie specialty shops that will do the fitting, suggesting you come at a time when they have few customers. Of course, bras purchased at such stores are more expensive. So you may have to simply measure him, take him to the discount or department store, and pick out ones you think will fit. He can always return them if they do not, explaining that they did not fit him properly. Select bras that are lightly padded since he has nothing to put in them at this time. Hormones, natural and synthetic as well as silicon glue-on attachments are readily available so you can get him a variety of sizes to suit your moods.

Now it's time for sissy's outerwear. When summer is almost over, it's a great time to purchase the short-shorts, tight tees, and tank tops he will be wearing now and next summer. Look for light colored short-shorts in white, yellow, and pink that will allow his flowered panties to show through. You will probably find them in the junior department since they are intended for teenage girls. The best styles have little holes in them with a liner. When you very carefully remove the liner with scissors, sissy will be wearing short-shorts with little holes that will show off his flower panties nicely. Be sure the panties have a light colored background and dark flowers for maximum effect.

Since these shorts will not likely have pockets, sissy will need a purse to carry his wallet, keys, sanitary pads, lipstick, and condoms. The condoms are there to make him wonder what's next. The purse should be small but distinctive and typically carried by teenagers. The color is up to you.

Sissy tees and tanks should also be light, pastel colors either solid or with designs that only a sissy would wear. They should fit tightly enough that his bra will show nicely. You may allow sissy to wear a ladies hat or baseball cap to keep the sun out of his eyes. Sunglasses may help hide his embarrassment.

Until he purchases sissy tennis shoes, his own may do. When he purchases his first sissy shoes, he will do so in a store where clerks help him, as described above. He will wear them out of the store, with his old shoes in the bag. Be sure his socks are distinctly sissy too with little designs that are color coordinated with his outfit.

When shopping, many people will have the opportunity to see sissy in his splendor, with his panties showing through his shorts and his lightly padded bra pressing out the tee or tank top and carrying his little purse, oooo so cute!

Domesticating Sissy

Since he wants to be your sissy, then from now on your sissy will do all the housework and the shopping that he can be trusted to do. Train him to shop for anything you want. He shall wait on you hand and foot. That's what a sissy does, so remind him of it if he questions you. Unless you have children or other adults in the home, he may do his house cleaning while wearing only his panties. Later, if you choose, he may be given a maid's outfit or some other clothing that you feel is appropriate to remind him of his sissy status.

There will be times when his cleaning is not what it should be. You should keep a hairbrush or paddle available for those occasions. If you choose to spank him while he is over your knee, be aware sissies have been known to cum while being spanked! If he is really bad, another punishment is to rub Ben Gay on his little cock and balls.

One approach to housework is to set up a schedule of chores for your sissy to do. In this way you both know what is to be done, when it must be completed and that failure will result in punishment.

This is what I personally recommend for the domestication of any sissy. It requires the sissy to, in addition to her other tasks, keep this schedule up and do it well. It allows you to add or subtract items as you may see fit. It makes the sissy completely responsible for her actions and consequences, not you. You are simply the administrator of the consequences for the failures of the sissy in performance of his duties!

In my case, I like my sissy restrained for weekly punishments. This allows me to punish at my leisure, over a longer period of time, with multiple instruments and as hard as I may choose.

For others, they may wish to do over-the-knee spankings and then send the sissy to stand in a corner to wait for you to be ready to start again.

Whatever application you may choose, punishment is a tool used to correct improper behavior in your sissy and instill the respect your sissy may be lacking for your position in life. But punishment need not be physical spanking alone but can be accompanied by humiliation. Or, depending upon your preferences, humiliation can be used as a replacement for physical punishment.

Below is the chore list and punishment chart I use for my sissy:

Lacie's Chore List

Weekly

Monday   Vacuum Upstairs & Dust

Tuesday   Vacuum Downstairs & Dust
                Empty All House Trash Cans
                Take Out Trash Cans to Curb

Wednesday   Wash Kitchen Floors
                Clean Sliding Glass Door
                Bring In Trash Cans from Curb

Thursday   Laundry - Wash, Iron & Put Away

Friday   Clean all Bathrooms, Tubs, Showers & Toilets

Every Other Week

Saturday or   Wash & Vacuum Mistress' Car
Sunday   Trim Front Yard Plants & Weed
                     Fertilize Lawn
                     Weed Back Yard

All chores must be completed by 6:00 PM on the day they are assigned.

Lacie's Punishment Chart

Quantity of Strokes	Offence
2	Not having candles lit by 7:00 PM
5	Wearing girl clothes without begging first
2	Not wearing girl clothing
2	Not wearing a bra
3	Not being completely dressed when we are alone
2	Not being in complete make-up when we are alone
5	Not wearing toenail polish
2	Not wearing fingernail polish
2	Toe or fingernail polish not in perfect shape
2	Not calling me Mistress when alone
10	Not reporting to me on time for our nights
2	Not having Mistress' panties out for her in the morning
2	Not having Mistress' toothbrush out for her in the morning
2	Not having Mistress' Q-Tip out for her in the morning
3	Not having Mistress' coffee for her in the morning
3	Not having Mistress' drink for her in the evening
5	Not doing a chore on time
8	Cumming without begging for permission
3	Not showering with Mistress
5	Not having a ribbon or chastity on your pathetic little dick
5	Not doing what I ask, when I ask
10	Not performing well on my pleasure nights
2	Not having perfume on
2	Not keeping body smooth & hair free
2	No lipstick on
2	Improper begging for anything

This is a daily penalty guide for possible offences. You can be penalized more than once each day for each offence. Mistress will keep track of the offences on a daily basis and administer the total of the above punishment strokes weekly on punishment night, with whatever implements she may choose, in whatever positions she may dictate.

Multiple implements used; in multiple positions; is a highly probable.

Sissy's Personal Rules

Every sissy needs your guidance, correction and understanding. This can be easily accomplished by setting up some simple personal rules your sissy must follow. Each sissy and sissy household is different so the rules you set should be tailored to your personal desires, needs, wants and household restrictions. Here is a simple set of personal care rules you can build on:

- Sissies must always wear panties. Sissies are not allowed to own men's underwear.
- Sissies do not cum without permission.
- Sissies wear a chastity device.
- Sissies must always have their toenails painted.
- When at work, sissies must always wear panties and have their toenails painted and any other feminine items that don't show.
- Sissies only sit to pee.
- Sissies shall have no body hair.
- Sissies shall have smooth soft skin at all times.
- Sissies use only female deodorant, shampoos, conditioners, soaps, etc.
- Sissies must perfume.
- Sissies should take frequent scented bubble baths.
- Sissies should always have well-manicured fingernails at all times and painted when possible.
- Sissies sit with knees together.
- Sissies must keep in shape by working out to an aerobics videotape while wearing a feminine leotard and tights at least three times a week.
- Sissies wear nightgown or some other type of feminine nightie to bed.
- Sissies subscribe to women's magazines and read them.

- Sissies when going out, other than to work, besides panties, will wear a bra and pantyhose under their clothing.
- Sissies shop, supervised, for their own clothes and get help from the sales staff. They must tell anyone that may ask that it is for them.
- When shopping for clothes, if offered a chance to try on clothes, take it. You should also always be wearing panties, pantyhose and a bra under your clothes when you go out looking for new clothes.

Sissy Reinforcement

From time to time a sissy may get complacent or lax in their duties. This is where punishment comes in, to remind them that their chosen path has consequences for unacceptable behavior. However, now that you have gotten used to the sissy lifestyle and are being treated like the Queen you really are, you don't want your sissy to change their minds. Even the threat of exposure may not always quell an uprising.

This is why I recommend, from time to time, you reinforce your sissy's desires and needs through arousal. Once you sexually arouse a sissy, they will do and say amazing things to cum. By exploiting this fact and tempting him and teasing him with sexy suggestiveness, you can have him on his knees begging you to allow him to kiss your feet, wait on you, clean for you, satisfy you sexually and even humiliate himself for you. Follow this procedure whenever you feel your hold on him is getting weak:

- Wearing your sexiest outfit, bring your sissy into the bedroom, sit on the bed and undress him.
- Ask him if he's been a good sissy for you as you run your fingernails between his thighs.
- Ask him to kneel down to rub your tired feet. Then tell him that he may kiss them if he wishes to. Allow him to kiss your feet, all the way up your legs, to the crux of your thighs.

- Turn around and have him give your bottom a kiss or two, to demonstrate his sincerity.

- Tie his hands behind his back. Then have him attempt to undress you with his mouth and teeth.

- Remove his chastity device.

- Don't let him touch or otherwise arouse himself. That's what those beautifully manicured fingernails of yours are for! Use them to keep him aroused.

- Now have him take his place at your feet while you read aloud a female domination story or two. The kind of story you know will keep his attention.

- While reading, keep him teased and aroused with your toes. Make sure he gets nice and hard, but only touch it when he needs prodding. Bring him to the brink, but don't let him release! Use this opportunity to manipulate him deeper into his submissive role. Make him confess his fetishistic desires and proclaim his adulation for you.

- Avail him to your now-musky panty crotch. Allow him to sniff, kiss and lick the outside of your panties. Again, have him confess his fetishistic desires and proclaim his adulation for you.

- Allow him to remove your panties with his teeth. Then pull his face toward into you. Tell him to kiss and lick only on your command. Issue these commands as if you were training a puppy. If he disobeys you, gag him with your panties and make him nuzzle you with his nose.

- When his session of oral servitude is complete to your supreme satisfaction, have him lie face up on the bed and tie his legs and arms to the bedposts.

- Straddle him. Sit on his chest and find out what he would do to be allowed to kiss your breasts. Hover over him. Get close enough for him to suckle your nipples, then pull away. Slap his face. Make him beg.

- Turn around and avail him to your bottom. Allow him to kiss your cheeks as you pinch and tickle his cock. Make him reach with the tip of his tongue to taste the fruit between your legs. Ask him if he's ready to assume the role of your "Personal Ass Kisser" for life. Let him audition for the role. Tell him that whether you make love to him that night depends on the lust and eagerness he exhibits in worshipping your nether hole.

- By this time, he should be ready to explode. So, naturally you'll want to take a break. Retire to the kitchen for a glass of wine, leaving him to ponder more ways in which he can please his new boss. Drape your moist panties over his face, to give him something to inspire him.

- When you return, give him a rousing massage between his legs, to stoke those fires within his loins.

- Verbal stimulation is often very effective, tell him things you might do to reward him, tease him with ideas you know he'd enjoy, threaten to humiliate him if he doesn't satisfy you.

- Ask questions about his desires and needs and tease him while he answers you.
- As you continue to tease him, have him come up with ways to serve you, ways you can punish him, what clothing he should wear, etc.

The key here is stimulation or arousal without letting him cum. Once in that excited, aroused state, you can ask anything and get an answer. Delve into his deepest desires and fantasies. Have him explain them to you in great detail, all the while keeping him aroused without a climax.

When you are ready, mount him and ride him to the hilt, repeating to him his desires and fantasies that you will be living out, with him as your sissy, as you bring him to a thundering orgasm!

You have accomplished reinforcement of his desires through sexual release. One of the most reliable personality changing techniques any women can use.

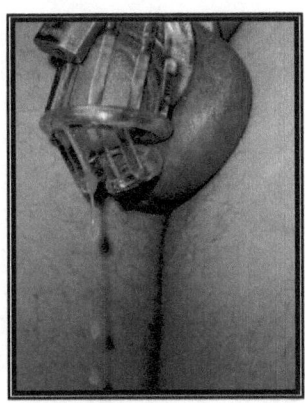

Sissy Chastity & Milking

All sissies should be in a chastity of some sort, as most are compulsive masturbators. There are many chastity device shops on line that you can order from. An ideal situation would be to have your sissy sit with you while you shop and discuss the various types, advantages, disadvantages, etc. When your order finally arrives, it should be installed as soon as possible.

The concept of a chastity device is that your sissy will no longer be in control of his own pleasure, you will. You will decide if and when he may cum. You will have complete control over the frequency, the method and the location of any sexual release. This makes you totally responsible for any sexual pleasure your sissy may have!

Because a chastity device restricts erection, it causes a little pain. This gives you another tool to use with your sissy. You can arouse your sissy without the removal of the device as a reminder of his status at any time, causing him a little pain, without ever laying a hand on him.

Another form of chastity for a sissy is a fermium loop. This is a metal band that is secured around the head of the sissy's penis to a pierced in place metal barbell. Sometimes the ends of the barbell are broken off or sealed on so that it cannot be removed. In this case, the sissy will no longer be able to experience any form of sexual release or perform as a male. With this device on, getting any form of erection causes pain and eventually the sissy's mind will cause erections to cease to avoid the pain.

If you do not want your sissy to have any pleasure during orgasm and you want to eliminate any nocturnal emissions, milking is a humiliating form of sissy release that can be easily accomplished while keeping his chastity in place. The process of milking a chastised sissy dry while denying her an orgasm provides you with the ultimate control over your sissy.

Most of the feeling from sex for a male is through the stimulation of the head and then the feeling of fluid being quickly released. To keep your sissy in check, you need to deny those feelings from the body and mind. To do this you must not let the penis become totally aroused and never stimulate the head. If your sissy has a chastity device on then this will be accomplished. If not, then a simple piece of cord, zip tie or shoelace tied around the penis several times will work. Do not tie it too tight as to cause the penis to lose all blood flow, just enough to make any emissions ooze out verses spurt out.

The actual milking of your sissy can become a more ritualistic process that is designed to remind your sissy of her status and humiliate at the same time. The period between milking is up to you.

The technique used is the prostate massage method, but the penis is not to be aroused or excited by touch, and remains locked within the chastity.

Prostate milking sometimes involves placing ice around the cock and balls to reduce the enjoyment. Inventive Mistresses and Masters have even designed homemade ice trays to freeze the water in a shape of a thick ice cock ring, which the chaste sissy must wear during the milking session.

The milking session usually lasts between 10 - 40 minutes, and is a pleasurable gentle massage of the prostate, after about 10 minutes you will begin to release fluid which has a sensation similar to slow urinating, after continued massage, the fluid flows out freely. Perhaps the fluid is collected as it drops in a jar, condom, cup or saucer. A good sissy will consume all of her man dribble, as a demonstration of her sissy slut status and a willingness to serve you.

The key factor to milking is that the semen should not be allowed to shoot from the head of the penis. This is where the pleasure in ejaculating lies. It should only be allowed to dribble slowly out the tip of the worthless flesh in question. If the flow is restricted and just dribbles out, the sissy will experience release without the pleasurable effects. This is the desired result for all sissy sluts, release without pleasure.

I recommend that a sissy slut always be in a chastity device and that milking is done while the sissy is restrained from movement with her ass in the air.

For my sissy slut milking ritual, I make my sissy slut get all of the items ready and wait for me at the foot of my bed. My items include a whip, wrist and ankle cuffs, rope, rubber gloves, ben-gay, a plate and large dildo. I make my sissy slut strip to her lingerie and remove her panties while I watch and verbally humiliate her. Then she must put on her wrist and ankle cuffs and kneel up on the bed. I then spread her feet wide apart and tie them to the foot board. Next, I'll pull her arms between her feet and tie her wrist cuffs to the foot board. I shove the plate under her worthless caged worm and warm her nicely exposed ass with my whip while I command that she beg me to milk her. I apply about eight or ten good hard blows, I like to hear her scream and moan for me while she begs. Then I'll put on the rubber gloves and really lube her well with the ben-gay. Inserting my finger in her now hot pussy hole, I'll slowly massage her prostrate as she repeats "I am your sissy, I am a slut, I want to serve you," until she dribbles all of her male juice out on to the plate. Now, a quick filling of her pussy hole with the dildo, a few pumps in and out, another six to eight strokes with the whip and she's done. I'll undo the rope and have her beg me to lick the plate clean while I watch and verbally abuse her some more. Then my sissy slut gets dressed, cleans all the items and puts them away for the next time.

As an occasional treat, you could remove the chastity and watch as the sissy is required to masturbate on a plate as you tease and verbally humiliate him. After your sissy is done, require him to beg you for permission to lick it all up!

For a sissy that is not kept in a chastity device, there are two on-the-spot methods you can use to bring your sissy's libido into balance. If, for example, your sissy is behaving in a particularly manic, agitated way, just pull her panties down and masturbate her. You'll relieve her of her excessive energy and calm her down immediately. This trick works every time. And if your sissy is withholding while you're trying to masturbate her, just put some lotion on your hand and insert the middle finger of your other hand up her ass. The effect is remarkable. Then, when all has been spewed, have her lick it all up. Of course you can always use a plate or cup to catch everything and then have her beg you to eat it all.

Another technique is used with sissies who are listless and cranky. You can perk such a sissy up right away by using the technique above, but forbidding her permission to ejaculate. The idea here is for you to force your sissy into a state of arousal and keep her that way for as long as possible. You'll find that dressing provocatively and talking sexy to her will help. Or you can always punish her if she cums without your express permission!

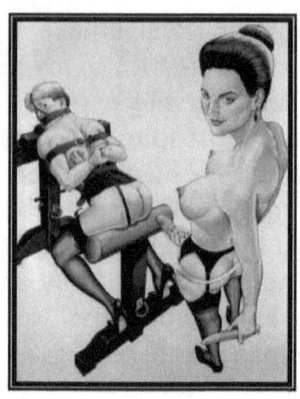

Sissy Control

Every sissy has to be controlled in some way. Often, punishment is not enough to reinforce the true sissy nature and keep him in check. There are many ways, in addition to and conjunction with punishment, to do this. Humiliation and cuckolding are other methods, which I go into in separate chapters, and dildo training, which I will discuss here.

Most every sissy wants to be ravaged by his Mistress and forced to do sexually obscene and degrading things. They want to be fully into the domestic female role and have their Mistress, while maintaining her femininity and sexiness, take on the male sexual role around them. They want to be *forced* to orally and physically serve their Mistress and become the household sissy maid, personal sissy assistant, sissy cuckold, or other sissy fantasy you may have discovered during your questioning. What great news, so enjoy it! Enjoy the pleasures of having a male that you can dress, tease and torment, at your discretion, which is always on call to pleasure you as you command, when you command it, and not receive pleasure for himself in return.

An aspect of this control is your ability to fully treat him like the sissy he wants to be by ramming your dildo into his new found pussy hole. Perhaps the ultimate form of control or punishment a Mistress can use on her sissy. To a growing number of women, the strap-on dildo is as essential to good home discipline and control of their sissies as any other form of punishment.

The device itself consists of a harness and straps that fit around a woman's waist along with a phallus, usually made of rubber or plastic. Most adult toy stores with a femme-centric emphasis stock a supply of strap-on appliances and accessories. It is well worth a Mistress time to take a sissy out and spend an afternoon deciding what kind of strap-on to buy. Just be sure to explain to the saleswoman that you are looking for a strap-on dildo to use on your sissy. She should be able to help you find one that is sturdy enough for the task of punishing a sissy slut from behind

How long do you take a sissy from behind? That is entirely up to you. You will probably tire before he does because you will be doing all the work. Some sissies climax from dildo play as the dildo rubs the prostate gland and if he is in chastity, he will have some pain from his straining erection too. Climaxing is no big deal if he is in a chastity because the pleasure he feels when he cums will be denied.

He will probably go limp during dildo play, so don't go by outward appearances. He will still experience some stimulation. Dildo play is usually uncomfortable and pleasurable at the same time to a man, but the effects on his mind are worth it. It is truly a submissive experience for a sissy to be taken by a woman in his pussy hole. Or the best, being forced to accept Mistress' lover in the ass while the Mistress watches!

There are many ways and places to take your sissy, be creative and experiment. From behind with him bent over a table or chair and his legs spread; with him on his back with his knees spread and tucked toward his head; on the bed, tied with you behind; on the bed tied with you in front, this depends if you want to see his face or not when you are doing it. There is also you lying on the bed and forcing him to ride you up and down too!

Once you get skilled and become comfortable doing this to him, you will experience a tremendous power rush. You will feel powerful and you will want to increase the speed and the force of the thrusts as you hold onto his hips with your hands. Some strap-on harnesses support a two-headed or dual dildo so a woman can insert the one side into her and the other into her submissive. That way she can experience physical pleasure as well as the mental satisfaction. There are even vibrating harnesses that can stimulate your clitoris as you take your sissy.

For many a sissy, the simple awareness that her Mistress keeps a strap-on at hand is enough to make her behave herself. A typical sissy can be made more obedient by the Mistress wearing a strap-on around the house; they will fit well over a swimsuit or cat suit. This will allow a Mistress to approach her sissy slut at will, demand the sissy slut remove her panties and bend over for some good old fashioned drilling. A

Mistress walking around with her strap-on at the ready will definitely keep a sissy's attention if she has been slack in her duties.

Most sissies will crave the use of a strap-on regularly, as part of the love making routine with a Mistress. A Mistress may emphasize a sissy's status by requiring her to dress up in stockings, garter belt, bra, high heels and full make-up, then making her "service" the strap-on, prior to love making. Such experiences are also beneficial for a Mistress to use on smart-talking sissies. There is no better antidote to a smart ass remark, than a strap-on dildo inserted in the mouth of the smart-aleck in question.

The strap-on isn't only a punitive device, however. It can be a tool used by a sissy to satisfy the needs of a Mistress too. The sissy is required to strap it on and make love to the Mistress all night long! This way the Mistress gets what they want and the sissy gets nothing except exercise!

A sissy that is wearing a butt plug of a decent size on a regular basis, the strap-on can be used almost all the time, at a moment's notice, to take the sissy with total abandon.

A Mistress can accomplish this by purchasing a locking dildo harness or demanding your sissy make one for his own use. Then insert butt plugs into the sissy's pussy hole and lock them in place with the harness, for extended periods of time, hours or days. Start off with a small plug and then after several hours, replace it with a bigger one, and so on until the desired size is easily accepted. Once you have reached your size goal, practice or wearing of the harness will be required, just not for as long a time as when you first started, and should be done multiple times each week.

Using a butt plug, locked in place, is a good form of punishment too.

Sissy Humiliation

Humiliation and a sissy go hand and hand. You can use humiliation as a form of punishment, status reminder and just for fun. But to fully keep your sissy in his place, humiliation must be used.

There are many ways a sissy can be made to suffer and humiliation is one of the easiest and most entertaining ways, which often goes a lot further than any other form of punishment a Mistress can devise.

Humiliation may take on many forms in your lifestyle. It is really up to you the Mistress to fully explore and develop the way this tool will be used in your relationship with your sissy. Depending upon who knows about his status, humiliation may begin with the informing of others and then expand to service in front of others and then later become service with others as a cuckold or a sex slave to males for amusement.

Humiliation is a treacherous tool in the sense that sissies can build-up immunity to the effects, causing the Mistress to expand and push the limits of her own personal tastes. However, it is a necessary and effective tool nonetheless. I have found that as my humiliation of my sissy continues, so does my creativeness, confidence and ability to try new forms of torment and degradation. It is sort of like getting in the shower, at first it may be a little warm, but then as prolonged exposure sets it, you turn up the temperature because you feel cool. The effect of humiliation is one and the same; what works today, after continued practice, may not always work tomorrow.

Now there are some basic things that every sissy should be doing, that is not really humiliation, but are required things that are dictated by his sissy status. They are as noted in previous chapters and are the *basics* of being a sissy. *Humiliation* is something that pushes all the boundaries of his male existence and even some of yours. It is the last thing your sissy would consider dreaming about or doing.

An example would be the Mistress taking on a lover and making the sissy, dressed in his best sissy outfit, serve the both of you as your personal maid, while being teased, verbally insulted and tormented by the both of you, during her service. Later, being forced to strip for the both of you down to her lingerie and then tied to a chair in the room where the two of you will have sex. Forced to watch you and your lover enjoy each other's pleasures, maybe even be forced to pleasure your lover orally while you verbally humiliate your sissy. Then, when you are through, your sissy is untied and forced to clean you and your lover of all spent juices. Maybe even have your lover punish your sissy in front of you before you re-tie him and the two of you begin your passion again.

Here are some basic ideas for sissy humiliation, but not the only ones for sure, and using your imagination you can certainly go in many different directions from mild to wild.

- Make him take a sewing class and learn to make lingerie for himself.
- Make him take a learning annex class on stripping, pole dancing or belly dancing to amuse you.
- Order him to visit the cosmetics department in a nice store where he has to ask the sales lady to help him buy foundation in his color.
- Have him set you up with different partners on a date, where he has to explain to them his position in the household. Maybe even serve the two of you drinks, dinner, etc.
- Have him go to a yardage store and buy the frilliest material available for the making of his new apron. Then have him take the material to a seamstress where he will have it sewn to his exact waist size. Of course he must try it on for fit before he leaves. You could even order him to have his "sissy name" embroidered on it.
- Make him ask the sales girl in a lingerie department to help him buy two pair of matching panties in different sizes; one for you and one for him.
- Order him to go to a Laundromat and wash your panties in the sink by hand. Then load them in the dryer and sit in front of it watching them dry. Once dry, he must take them out and fold them in front of everyone.
- Have him get a manicure or pedicure. Of course he will need to have his nails painted in your favorite shade.
- Take him to try on lady's wigs and maybe even buy one and wear it out.

- Send him to a tanning salon and make him tan wearing only a sexy bikini so he can develop nice dark bikini tan lines.
- Take him to a lingerie store or the lingerie section of a department store and have him ask the sales lady if she has a sexy teddy that would fit him. Maybe he could try it on too!
- Make him go to a pharmacy where he has to buy an enema syringe, K Y Jelly, sanitary napkins, a red lipstick, and a condom all in the same purchase. Make sure all items are on one receipt.
- Other humiliation ideas:
  After orgasm, making sub drink his own cum; Always address a superior as Mistress or Master; Anal plugs; Baby pacifier tied around neck; Bathroom use control; Bathroom use in front of others; Carrying a doll or toy around; Clip on earrings that don't match; Cum or urinate into their food; Curtsy in public; Dom chooses food; Dom chooses clothes; Dom urinates into water while sub is taking a bath; Eat from a pet dish; Eat from floor; Eat without utensils; Enema; Eye contact restrictions; Feed submissive from hand; Feminine jewelry on; Foot worship; Forced exercising; Forced nudity; Forced masturbation in odd places; Forced to go to bathroom in front of others; Forced to sell lemonade in the street like a kid for 10 cents; Forced to wear a sign (slut, etc.); Forced to wear a leash; Golden shower; Handcuffs in public; Handcuffed to a shopping cart while shopping; Hired out as a maid for income; Lead on leash while having a rubber bone in the mouth for a walk; Leave bathroom door opened; Leave note with embarrassing instructions; Made to urinate in front of others into a cat litter box; Maid services for friends; Make sub wear underwear that you've urinated on; Nipple clamps under see thru top; Orgasm control; Orgasm denial; Pantyhose under shorts; Scolding; Spitting in face; Send shopping with note and hand it to clerk; Serve others (supervised); Serve others (unsupervised); Serve as toilet; Slap face; Slave tattoos (temporary); Spanking (public); Stand in corner; Swallow urine (own and or Mistress' / Master's); Suck dildo in car, so others can see; Make Video; Verbal Abuse; Wear diapers; Wear cum on face without wiping; Wear bra under see thru top; Wear panties under see thru pants / shorts; Wear T-shirt that says "I'm a sissy boy"; Wear Collar everywhere; Wear chastity device; Write on body (slut, sissy, etc.); Undress in front of others.

Sissy Contracts

Some Mistress' may wish to have more than an *oral* agreement with their sissy. They may desire a ceremony or a written agreement that spells out what the rules the sissy will have to follow and how they will be punished if they don't. We have given you a basic ritualistic ceremony earlier in the book but let's not forget about a second wedding ceremony where you both are the brides or he is the sissy bride and you are the executive wife-groom. This is always exciting and provides for a great get together of friends and associates that your sissy may serve throughout the party.

Contracts can be used instead of a ceremony or in conjunction with a ceremony. Be creative and write your own agreement keeping in mind the following points as a minimum:

- Identify who the parties are and the roles they will maintain.
- Identify what each party's responsibilities are in the new relationship.
- Identify what will happen to either party they fail in their responsibilities.
- Identify a time period this relationship will continue for before a review.
- All parties sign and date. You may also have witnesses sign too!

To get your ideas going, I have provided you with a copy of my agreement between my sissy and myself:

The Mistress – slave Agreement

Be it hereby known to all that (   ) desires to become a feminized panty slave and sex toy to a woman and (   ) desires to have a male to do her bidding and be under her total sexual control.

Therefore, both (   ), hereinafter referred to as Mistress and (   ), hereinafter referred to as slave, have come together under this contract and agree to the following terms and conditions:

ollateral

The slave agrees to be photographed in various articles of clothing and in various ways, in bondage, being punished, etc., as istress desires and sees fit. Those photographs will be sealed in preaddressed envelopes, along with this agreement, to his peers and friends. Those envelopes shall then be stored in a secure location so that no accidental mailing or discovery can occur. In the event the slave is found to be in default of this contract, those letters shall be mailed out.

efinitions

The term istress shall be defined as the person in charge of all aspects of the slave. Not limited to, but shall include control of sexual activity, discipline, training, transformation, apparel, humiliation and degradation. It is she that chooses what, how and when punishment of the slave is administered. It is she that dictates what the slave is to wear. It is she that is responsible for the feminization of said slave and the exposure of that feminization to others. It is she that forces the slave to do her bidding by administering punishments to her fullest extent. The term slave shall be defined as the person that gives up control of all sexual activity and desires to the istress. The person that follows istress' commands to the fullest extent possible with the understanding that failure will be met with punishment. This person shall accept all punishment, humiliation and degradation from the Mistress, without question, when and where Mistress commands and desires.

ecitals

Mistress shall have the obligation to feminize her slave which may include but shall not be limited to, having her slave wear female undergarments of various descriptions at all times; removing all his body hair, except head hair; tattooing in nonpublic spots; body piercing in nonpublic spots; having pedicures and manicures; keeping toenails painted; dressing in female clothing; dressing in suggestive or skimpy clothing or outfits; leather; pvc or vinyl; body or other jewelry; using a female name; regular anal sex by Mistress or others; breast enlargement; hormones; forced same sex oral and or anal service; penis reduction, restriction or confinement; makeup; wigs; lingerie wearing and body sculpting.

Mistress has the right to select what clothing the slave may wear at any given time.

Mistress has the right to provide slave with specific and or general tasks, daily or otherwise, to perform as directed. Failure to do so shall result in punishment.

Mistress has the right to have other sexual partners. To this extent, Mistress may elect to have her slave service them during these encounters. The slave shall perform as Mistress sees fit and shall not refuse a command. Failure shall result in punishment.

Punishment of the slave is under the discretion of the Mistress and shall be delegated for breaking of the rules and/or for the enjoyment of the Mistress. Punishment shall include but not be limited to being tied up; heavy bondage; gagging; branding; spanking; whipping; dildos; prostitution; drinking urine; butt plugs; forced enlargement of anus; eating feces; homosexuality; eating cum; humiliation; degradation; anal sex; cock and ball torture; nipple torture; hot wax; diapers; plastic panties; racks or stocks and suspension. Since it is pleasurable for Mistress to punish her slave, the slave shall obey at all times and may be subjected to punishment 'just because'. The slave shall submit to all punishments directed by Mistress, whether administered by Mistress or others. The slave never has the right to refuse punishment, however punishment maybe postponed to a later date upon Mistress' agreement.

Training of the slave may include the talents of others as Mistress may see fit. This may include but not be limited to other Masters or Mistress' or both; other couples; professional slave training schools; professional Mistress' video tapes, audio, books, computers, stories and web sites.

Humiliation and degradation of the slave for Mistress' pleasure shall include but not be limited to denial of sexual release for long periods; release in the presence of others; chastity devices; going out in public as a female; going out in public as a slave; serving as a slave to others; homosexual service; prostitution; purchasing and trying on of female apparel; wearing unisex clothing; wearing tampons; wearing diapers; wearing plastic panties; maintaining a more feminine hairstyle; public spanking; eating own cum; wearing butt plug; enlarging anus; serving as a toilet; wearing female beach attire; wearing suggestive clothing; wearing a wig; jewelry; serving as a maid and pleasuring Mistress' other sexual partners.

The slave shall at all times seek out new ways to please Mistress and new ways that Mistress may punish, humiliate and feminize him.

The slave acknowledges that he has a tiny, insignificant, worthless cock and that its only use is for pleasuring his Mistress. The slave shall not touch or otherwise stimulate his tiny, worthless cock without the permission of the Mistress and shall never ejaculate without her consent. Failure to comply shall result in punishment and if Mistress so desires, strict chastity training which may include a full time chastity device.
The slave must consume any ejaculate that comes from his worthless little cock, in any way Mistress may see fit.

The slave shall, within six months after date below, be able to cum from anal sex without any other stimulation. Failure to accomplish this task will result in harsher punishment and humiliation until this can be done.

The slave shall, within six months after date below, be able to fit comfortably into a size 16 and begin to develop a more feminine figure. Failure to do so will result in corset training until this is accomplished.

The slave shall, within twelve months after date below, be able to fit comfortably into a size 14 and further develop a feminine figure. Failure to do so will result in harsher punishments and humiliation along with stricter corset training.

The slave shall satisfy the Mistress with his cock, orally, by the use of his hand, a strap on or a vibrator, all at the Mistress' discretion. When Mistress desires insertion of the slave's tiny, worthless cock, the slave shall maintain an erection in order to perform. Mistress may allow slave to ejaculate inside of her but will require all residue to be immediately cleaned out with slave's mouth. Failure to maintain an erection, clean Mistress properly or satisfy the Mistress is cause for punishment.

If at any time Mistress fails to fulfill the required tasks within this contract, she shall receive a written warning that she is in breach and will upon receipt of that warning correct said breach within 24 hours. Failure to do so shall void this contract. If voided by Mistress, slave shall have the right to have Mistress vacate the premises and have no further contact with her.

If at any time slave fails to submit for punishment as allowed within this contract, he shall receive a written warning that he is in breach and will upon receipt of that warning correct said breach within 24 hours. Failure to do so shall void this contract. If voided by the slave, Mistress shall mail aforementioned

collateral out to slave's associates. Mistress reserves the right, at her discretion, to stay and continue in the relationship. If this should occur, the slave shall provide another form of acceptable collateral.

It is understood that no activity shall interfere with the employment of either party, or any friend or acquaintance not in the same or similar lifestyle.

Further, Mistress may at her discretion, involve other people

that are in the same or similar lifestyles or friends of Mistress' and attend special events or functions without being in breach of this agreement and without consulting the slave.

It is understood that the terms of this contract may only be changed or the entire contract dissolved by mutual consent.

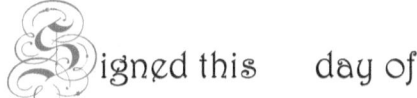igned this   day of

By:

Mistress

sissy slave

Sissy Exercise

HEIGHT AND WEIGHT TABLES FOR WOMEN
According to Frame, Ages 25-59
Weight in Pounds (In Indoor Clothing)*

HEIGHT		SMALL	MEDIUM	LARGE
(In Shoes)+		FRAME	FRAME	FRAME
Feet	Inches			
4	10	102-111	109-121	118-131
4	11	103-113	111-123	120-134
5	0	104-115	113-126	122-137
5	1	106-118	115-129	125-140
5	2	108-121	118-132	128-143
5	3	111-124	121-135	131-147
5	4	114-127	124-138	134-151
5	5	117-130	127-141	137-155
5	6	120-133	130-144	140-159
5	7	123-136	133-147	143-163
5	8	126-139	136-150	146-167
5	9	129-142	139-153	149-170
5	10	132-145	142-156	152-173
5	11	135-148	145-159	155-176
6	0	138-151	148-162	158-179

- Indoor clothing weighing 5 pounds for men and 3 pounds for women.
- + Shoes with 1-inch heels

HEIGHT AND WEIGHT TABLES FOR MEN

According to Frame, Ages 25-59
Weight in Pounds (In Indoor Clothing)*

HEIGHT	SMALL	MEDIUM	LARGE
(In Shoes)+	FRAME	FRAME	FRAME
Feet Inches			
5 2	128-134	131-141	138-150
5 3	130-136	133-143	140-153
5 4	132-138	135-145	142-156
5 5	134-140	137-148	144-160
5 6	136-142	139-151	146-164
5 7	138-145	142-154	149-168
5 8	140-148	145-157	152-172
5 9	142-151	148-160	155-176
5 10	144-154	151-163	158-180
5 11	146-157	154-166	161-184
6 0	149-160	157-170	164-188
6 1	152-164	160-174	168-192
6 2	155-168	164-178	172-197
6 3	158-172	167-182	176-202
6 4	162-176	171-187	181-207

Indoor clothing weighing 5 pounds for men and 3 pounds for women.

+ Shoes with 1-inch heels

Now that you have an idea what the height to weight ration based upon the frame size should be, add into the mix, the personal Body Mass Index (BMI). Below is a table, according to a variety of weights and heights, which can give you this index number.

The BMI is a number that represents a reliable indicator of fat amassed in a body base upon height and weight.

Numbers without any underline represents a good BMI.

Numbers with a light gray underline represents an acceptable BMI but could use some reduction.

Numbers with a dark gray underline represents an unacceptable BMI. A sissy will need to exercise more and lose some weight to pull the BMI in line.

Therefore, even if the height to weight ratio, based upon frame size, is within an acceptable range, the BMI may indicate a need to bring more exercise into sissy's daily routine.

Body Mass Index (BMI), kg/m² * WEIGHT (lbs)

Body mass index (BMI) according to a variety of weights and heights.

The BMI is calculated by dividing weight in kilograms by height in meters squared. For example, a person who weighs 180 lbs and is 5'5" would have a BMI of 30

	120	130	140	150	160	170	180	190	200	210	220	230	240	250	260	270	280	290	300	310	320
4'10"	25	27	29	31	34	36	38	40	42	44	46	48	50	52	54	57	59	61	63	65	67
4'11"	24	26	28	30	32	34	36	38	40	43	45	47	49	51	53	55	57	59	61	63	65
5'0"	23	25	27	29	31	33	35	37	39	41	43	45	47	49	51	53	55	57	59	61	63
5'1"	23	25	27	28	30	32	34	36	38	40	42	44	45	47	49	51	53	55	57	59	61
5'2"	22	24	26	27	29	31	33	35	37	38	40	42	44	46	48	49	51	53	55	57	59
5'3"	21	23	25	27	28	30	32	34	36	37	39	41	43	44	46	48	50	51	53	55	57
5'4"	21	22	24	26	28	29	31	33	34	36	38	40	41	43	45	46	48	50	52	53	55
5'5"	20	22	23	25	27	28	30	32	33	35	37	38	40	42	43	45	47	48	50	52	53
5'6"	19	21	23	24	26	27	29	31	32	34	36	37	39	40	42	44	45	47	49	50	52
5'7"	19	20	22	24	25	27	28	30	31	33	35	36	38	39	41	42	44	46	47	49	50
5'8"	18	20	21	23	24	26	27	29	30	32	34	35	37	38	40	41	43	44	46	47	49
5'9"	18	19	21	22	24	25	27	28	30	31	33	34	36	37	38	40	41	43	44	46	47
5'10"	17	19	20	22	23	24	26	27	29	30	32	33	35	36	37	39	40	42	43	45	46
5'11"	17	18	20	21	22	24	25	27	28	29	31	32	34	35	36	38	39	41	42	43	45
6'0"	16	18	19	20	22	23	24	26	27	29	30	31	33	34	35	37	38	39	41	42	43
6'1"	16	17	19	20	21	22	24	25	26	28	29	30	32	33	34	36	37	38	40	41	42
6'2"	15	17	18	19	21	22	23	24	26	27	28	30	31	32	33	35	36	37	39	40	41

* Conversion Factors:
Weight in lbs/2.2 = weight in kilograms (kg) : Height in inches x 0.0254 = height in meters (m) : 1 foot = 12 inches

Now that you have ascertained the correct information for your sissy's personal body type, you may need to increase her exercise level to achieve it.

Even if you are already at a good level, daily exercise will help keep her toned and fit, thus able to please you more fully.

Have your sissy buy herself a good workout DVD, video or join a gym. Keep in mind a sissy's exercise program should be designed for females only.

A sissy should have a leotard, matching tights, socks and shoes to exercise in! Maybe even some sweat bands as accessory accents to complete the outfit. One variation on a leotard is a one piece swimsuit. Make it as feminine as possible, with not too tight of a fit. Pantyhose can double for tights too! Use ribbed elasticized socks to protect them from runs. When shopping remember that actually trying on an item your sissy is considering purchasing is the best way to check its fit. Having your sissy look herself in the mirror so she may see how it fits her body type and showing you how flattering it looks is always a thrill!

A humiliating thing for a good little sissy slut to do would be to join an all-female gym. You can accomplish this by contacting the owner or instructor and explaining to them your training, desires and goals. They may have your sissy explain themselves in front of the class they will attend and have the members vote on allowing her in. They may have your sissy attend at a time when no one else will be in and instruct her personally. They also may be so repulsed by the idea and what you have to say that they will tell you and your sissy to get out and never return again!

Sissy Playtime

All work and no play makes for one dull day in the life of any Mistress. So what's a Mistress to do?

Well, play with her sissy of course! He's close and you can tease, humiliate, punish and abuse him without any worries because he's your sissy! He wants needs and craves it! His life revolves around his Mistress, her bidding, her amusement and being her total toy! So let's all go play with our toys!

One fun thing any woman can do with a man that wants to be her sissy is turn him into the perfect 1950's American wife. Just like on the old television shows; Father Knows Best, Leave it to Beaver, The Donna Reid Show, Etc., just to name a few.

First, make him dress the part. High heels, stockings, girdle, full-length bra, short sleeve crisp cotton dress with a high collar, wide matching belt, short curled wig, full petty coat, flawless make-up and a waist apron.

Next, have him stay home from work and do all the washing, ironing - even if there is no need to iron, vacuuming, housecleaning and fixing of the typical 50's pot roast dinner. He should have a cocktail in hand and greet you at the door, looking fresh and domesticated when you get home.

Now he serves the dinner, makes small talk, dotes on your every word, cleans the table, does the dishes by hand wearing nice pink Playtex gloves and serves desert to you while you enjoy the paper or a bit of TV.

At the end of the evening, he changes into a long, full nightgown in a pastel color or white and then seductively comes in to get you and escorts you into the bedroom. In the bedroom he will undress you, pull back the sheets and lick, suck and eat you to multiple organisms. All the while you do nothing but enjoy. When he has completely satisfied you to your hearts content, he gets into bed and you roll over and go to sleep! As an added bonus, before he gets you undressed, you could always put him over your knee for a quick spanking if dinner, your cocktail or the house wasn't in perfect order upon your arrival!

Now, a variation of the above is the French Maid. The object and the play is exactly the same except the attire is that of a sexy, seductive maid.

With French Maid play, part of your roll is to supervise your maid clean and correct her poor performance with a paddle or ridding crop. The French Maid costume avails itself to this correction by the nature of its design, short, short skirt with ruffled panties peeking out. Of course, necessary Mistress servicing can also interrupt any cleaning project.

Another added spice on either of the above would be if your sissy served both you and your lover! Ou la la now that's French!

 And for the Mistress that prefers to stay monogamous, your sissy can do the above for any party you may want to have. If you should have concerns about the partygoer's impression of your sissy when they see him, make it a costume party! That will provide him an excuse to treat you like a goddess and dress like you demand, without giving away too much, too soon.

For a really cool play party, where people are coming that know about your sissy, you could always gag him with a ball gag or a pair of your dirty panties and wrap him completely in plastic food wrap. Then, lay him on the center of the main table and put the food around him to create the perfect sissy centerpiece.

To add some spice to the party, wrap everything but your sissy's ass cheeks in the plastic wrap. Place him ass up on the table with the food around but add a crop or paddle to the table with a note, instructing your guests to use them on your sissy's ass as they want to!

One idea, that may quickly become your favorite, is to dress your sissy in any way you choose. For this idea, dressing your sissy like a sissy slut works best and once you have him dressed like a total slut, dress yourself simple and nice. Now drive the two of you to a local gay bar and stop in for drinks. All you will have to do is sit back and watch the fun!

A variation on this would be to take your sissy to a lesbian bar and let the girls have their way with him! This may be worse than the gay bar for your sissy but still very fun for any Mistress.

The big girl sissy look is always a good time for any Mistress too. Dress your sissy up like a three-year-old little girl for the day or even the weekend. Feed her, show her off, take her out for walks, etc. all dressed like perfect little girl.

In addition to disciplining your little girl, you can be forced to put her back into diapers because of poor behavior! Little girls sometimes need to be put in their proper place.

Another fun treat for a Mistress would be to make your sissy take stripper lessons and then put on a show for you and or your friends, both male and female. They could put fake money in his little G-string and make him get their drinks between sets, just like at a real club!

Having a party in general and turning your sissy into a decorated room ornament is always a kick. Especially if your sissy has to explain himself to each guest when they inquire about what is going on. You could even place a placard at your sissy's feet explaining his position and gag him so he can't respond.

And of course, every Mistress always has the basic everyday humiliation items as listed in a previous chapter. Items so described can always be done just for the fun and amusement of any Mistress. They're a great day brightener for any Mistress. And don't forget about verbal humiliation. Telling your sissy in no uncertain terms how worthless they are to you, how pathetic their penis is, how they may never cum again, laughing at them in their panties and outfits, telling them how they will be required to serve you in the future, etc. are all good ideas for verbal humiliation. That is of course besides making fun of them whenever you can and teasing them about being a sissy and their status in the home with you.

Like being your toilet and sucking your pee from you as the need arises. Or, for the shy Mistress, watching her sissy drink Mistress pee from a glass that she has filled.

Make your sissy suck your lover's cock and then clean you afterwards.

Tie your sissy and gag him with your dirty panties, then whip him throughout the night while you leisurely read or watch TV.

Use a strap-on and wildly fuck him in the ass while he begs for it.

Tie him nude and put clothespins all over his body and then whip them off.

Make him keep a dildo in his ass all day.

Make him dress up for you and wash all your lingerie by hand. Now have him hang it out to dry in the back yard.

Have him build you a spanking horse so you can tie him to it so he can be punished.

Have him make you a whip you can use on him.

If you allow your sissy to squirt his juices now and then, make a game out of it. Have him play with himself and cum on a plate while you time him. Of course when he has cum he must beg you for permission to lick the plate clean. Then, have him do it all over again, only faster than his previous time. If he can't he gets whipped, one stroke for each 30 seconds, ten seconds, whatever time increment you feel like using, longer it takes him to cum over the first time. And of course, he must beg you to lick it all up!

Instead of regular boring old television one night, you can watch

sissy television. Have him act out something from a movie or book and then end it with a sex scene where your sissy must dildo himself in front of you while you verbally humiliate and taunt him as he rams himself with the dildo.

These are just some of the fun things any Mistress can do with their sissy. Be creative, enjoy it and remember to please yourself or command your sissy to do it for you!

Lastly, punishment of your sissy for your personal pleasure is a great experience. To restrain your sissy in various positions for extended periods of time and then whip them or apply clips to their bodies to make them squirm is fun, fun, fun! Go ahead and experiment, make them degrade themselves in a multitude of ways to please you. Sissies are very willing to please upon command. I have developed a game that you can play with your sissy along the punishment theme. It is available from me via email and comes with a starter set of 26 game cards, 2 unique dice and instructions. Additional sets of 20 cards with an additional die can also be purchased to create an 86 card total game, enough different and challenging tasks, ideas and various things to keep any sissy and Mistress quite happy.

Sissy Sex

Sex with a sissy can be interesting and enjoyable. It just depends upon the Mistress frame of mind and what her needs are.

Let us assume that you have your sissy in a chastity device of some sort. Without releasing him, you can tease and torment him over and over knowing full well he is experiencing some sort of pain and frustration from your caresses. Keep this up as often and for as long as you want until you are ready to have him orally service you without any release for himself.

Now on the occasion you want more than just his tongue, but without allowing him the pleasure of a climax, you have a few additional choices. Some chastity devices have an attachment that will allow for the insertion of a dildo right onto them. In this way he can perform all of the functions you enjoy and pound you until you can barely walk, without providing any genital pleasure for him. Thus, leaving your sissy, frustrated, horny and unsatisfied!

Another way to use your sissy that is in a chastity device is to have him put on your strap-on and use it on you. Again, like above, providing you with all the pleasure you can take and leaving your sissy frustrated, horny and unsatisfied!

Naturally, if you have a sissy that is not in chastity, you can put him in a girdle, a real tight pair of panties or a swimsuit bottom and have him tuck his worthless dangling member back between his legs. Then have him put on your strap-on to service your needs. This provides you with the pleasure and your sissy with nothing but exercise, which he may need anyway.

You can always use a double head dildo too. This is an extra-long dildo with a head at both ends. Put one end in his ass and the other in your pussy and go for it. If he is in a chastity device then this will be like milking him, if he is fortunate enough to be able to cum. You can use him for hours like this, until you can't take anymore!

Lastly, you can always buy a mouth gag that has a small penis shaped object at one end, the gag, and a larger, thicker shaped penis at the other, the dildo. Between the two is an attached strap and buckle to go around your sissy's head. This device eliminates all genital stimulation to your sissy and he is forced to use his head to bob up and down, back and forth, between your legs to satisfy your needs. This is a real fun sissy toy and I think every Mistress should add this to her collections!

A nice bit of torture you can do with a sissy in a chastity device or just a very tight fitting girdle is to have him take a penal stimulant, Viagra or other herbal mixture, and then tease him only without allowing him to cum or get fully erect! Oh what fun!

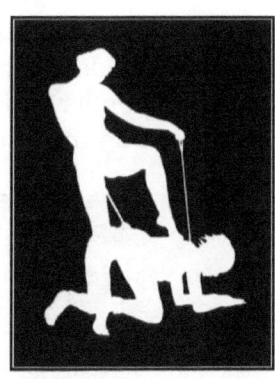

A Final Sissy Thought

To have anyone share their most private and personal thoughts with another, are special events. It is not every day another person will tell you their inner most desires and how much those desires revolve around pleasing you in some way while they are humbled, humiliated and even punished for their imperfections.

When you have a sissy, this is what they have done. Shared their most personal thoughts, feelings and fantasies with another person and have left themselves them totally exposed to you. You now have the control, the power and the ability to explore a new chapter in your relationship. Together you can go to a place in your bond that only a handful of people in relationships will ever get to. You will develop total trust and deeper feelings for one another as you explore this path. In no other relationship will you find such an exposure of one partner to another than a sissy to his Mistress.

Sure, he gets what he wants, the dressing up, being dominated, domesticated and controlled by you. But you now have an individual completely dedicated and compliant to you, your wellbeing, your happiness and your deepest sexual fantasies. Anything you want and you are in control.

So I say to all those who have discovered or had their partners confess to them these desires, enjoy! Live life as if there were no tomorrow for this is a new beginning that can open up many pleasurable doors, with you in the driver's seat and your partner at your side. Remember, you still have that same individual you have always known, trusted, loved and that has cared for you, whom you now just know even more intimate things about. And are his desires any different than the vanilla man who wants to open his own business, build his own hot rod, go hunting, run with the bulls or ride in a bicycle race, just to name a few? It's still the same person that you have always known, but better now because you really know what's on the inside.

Have Fun!

www.ingramcontent.com/pod-product-compliance
Lightning Source LLC
Chambersburg PA
CBHW050521290526
45786CB00007B/2649